# Herbs for the Holidays

# HERBS
## for the
# HOLIDAYS

## A Treasury of Decorations

### SAL GILBERTIE

*Photographs by George Ross*

*A Garden Way Publishing Book*

Storey Communications, Inc.
Schoolhouse Road
Pownal, Vermont 05261

*Edited by Gwen W. Steege*

*Cover and text design by Cynthia McFarland*

*Illustrated by Brigita Fuhrmann*

Garden Way Publishing was founded in 1973 as part of the Garden Way Incorporated Group of Companies, dedicated to bringing gardening information and equipment to as many people as possible. Today the name "Garden Way Publishing" is licensed to Storey Communications, Inc., in Pownal, Vermont. For a complete list of Garden Way Publishing titles call 1-800-827-8673. Garden Way Incorporated manufactures products in Troy, New York, under the Troy-Bilt® brand including garden tillers, chipper/shredders, mulching mowers, sicklebar mowers, and tractors. For information on any Garden Way Incorporated product, please call 1-800-345-4454.

*Printed in the United States by Semline, Inc.*

*Casebound by Book Press, Inc.*

*Color filmwork by Excelsior Printing Company*

*First Printing, July 1993*

**Library of Congress Cataloging-in-Publication Data**

Gilbertie, Sal.
    Herbs for the holidays : a treasury of decorations / Sal Gilbertie.
          p.      cm.
    Includes bibliographical references and index.
    ISBN 0-88266-871-4
    1. Holiday decorations.    2. Herbs—Utilization.    I. Title.
TT900.H6G54    1993
745.594'12—dc20        93-15282
                CIP

# Dedication

For our family and friends,
who have shared the joys,
laughter, and excitement
of so many wonderful
holidays at
47 Burr

# CONTENTS

# Acknowledgements

The love, support, and talents of many people made this book a reality. My special thanks to:

Marie Gilbertie, my wife, whose passion for perfection has inspired me in all my work.

Angela Miller, who believed in this book so much she sold it, not once, but twice! Her support and patience were especially appreciated during the long, hectic days of photography for the book.

Coleen O'Shea, whose professionalism never ceases to amaze me, and whose insights and perceptions contributed greatly to this project.

George Ross, for his beautifully lit photography and his even hand and calming manner during the long sessions we spent together.

Cathy Schwing, George's able assistant, for her heightened sense of color and style, and bottomless bag of props.

The staff at Storey Communications, especially my editor, Gwen Steege, who had faith in the book and its potential.

Larry Sheehan, for contributing his writing skills and for welcoming me at Bear River Farm when I needed a break.

Lois Russell, a decorator and artist who frequently came to my rescue with her friendship and talent.

Doris Romano, a loyal employee always willing to share her clever ideas and creations.

Tom Gilbertie, my son, for always being there for me, and especially for his love and concern for my well being.

To the entire crew at Gilbertie's, in the greenhouses and offices, in production and shipping, who make things happen, day in and day out, with dedication and hard work.

Maria Calise, a baker's baker, whose genius with a pastry bag kept us amazed — and full — all during the project.

Diane Tantimonico, for transcribing all my work tapes, while providing a much needed sense of humor at all the right times.

Bob Weiss and Steve Barrett for reminding me of my blessings.

Nick Nardi, for being a real live St. Nicholas in my life for so many years.

Without all these people, *Herbs for the Holidays* would not have been possible. Thank you, Lord, for making my life so full.

*Rustic Spray of Herbs and Greens*

Welcome

*G*loriously fragrant herb decorations, seasonings, and gifts
have for many years played a starring role at Christmastime
for the Gilbertie family. These marvelously scented visual
feasts, which add so much warmth and homespun charm
to our home, help our family not only to enjoy and appre-
ciate the holiday season, but also to share our joy with
others during this special time of year. From the beginning
of Thanksgiving festivities, through the next four weeks of
Advent, until Christmas itself, I am busy creating and
displaying the herb decorations that renew the thrill of
holidays for both children and adults.

One of the highlights of the season for my wife, Marie, and me is our annual Christmas Eve supper for the entire Gilbertie clan. For this event, as for others throughout the entire holiday season, herbs and their meanings play an important role. Although we call it "supper," our get-together on Christmas Eve is more in the nature of a banquet, for which we all get dressed up and sit at an attractively set formal table. For the table centerpiece, I use the Advent Wreath of cedar, boxwood, and holly, combined with bay, rosemary, golden thyme, lamb's-ears, purple sage, and tricolor sage, which I made earlier in the month (page 63). For this occasion, however, I replace its pink and purple candles with white candles, and I add fresh white roses, white daisies, and eucalyptus to it. At the place settings for all the women guests, I set out a white or red rose along with three or four sprigs of herbs, usually thyme (for courage), sage (for longevity), rosemary (for remembrance), and parsley (for festivity). When we all sit down, I take a moment to remind everyone of the symbolic associations of those herbs — just to sound a brief serious note before our celebration begins. The dinner itself is a fish-lover's feast in the Italian tradition, taken to perfection by Marie. Seven varieties of fresh seafood are prepared according to savory, old family recipes (see pages 70–71).

The Christmas Eve dinner culminates several busy and satisfying weeks in the Gilbertie house. Our enjoyment of the holiday season really begins as early as Thanksgiving weekend with the arrival of an annual unseen visitor we call "Big Turkey." This benevolent character brings the children of the family pomegranates, prickly pears, persimmons, and chocolate candy. We leave slices of toast and a handful of corn kernels for Big Turkey, and he invariably eats most of the snack — just as Santa Claus has room for all the milk and cookies left for him on Christmas Eve every year.

Big Turkey's visit is my signal to begin preparations for Christmas in earnest. Although I do some different things every year, I always spread the workload by making

*Table set for Christmas Eve ⇒*

sure to complete one or two herbal arrangements a night, beginning with the first weekend in December. Each morning, the younger children in the family get a kick out of seeing what new additions I've made to the decor.

For our family room, the arrangements I make are somewhat casual and humorous in concept and execution; in other rooms, they are quite formal. Sometimes an idea doesn't pan out. For instance, one year I strung red glass cardinals throughout the house on fishing line. Everybody shook their heads and said I had cluttered the ceilings with unconvincing birds. As I've refined my ideas and techniques over the years, I've made each project simpler, and I'm therefore more certain of success. That's why I'm confident that all the projects in this book, while they may appeal to the professional decorator, are well within the grasp of the inexperienced craftsperson, too.

Harvesting herbs from garden and farm is a joy throughout the growing season. Putting them to use in the home in so many beautiful and savory ways at Christmastime, when here in Connecticut all growth in the plant kingdom has come to a halt, is a deeply satisfying pleasure. I sincerely hope my herbal creations will help to bring love, merriment, and beauty to your home and family in the Christmas season.

*Lamb's-ears and yarrow hung to dry*

C H A P T E R   1

# An Herbal Workshop

*I*f you have ever worked with dried or fresh flowers, you will
have no trouble working with either dried or fresh herbs.
Here are a couple of simple pointers. To make dry or brittle
herbs more pliable, wrap them loosely in a dampened dish
towel overnight, or empty out the produce drawer in your
refrigerator and keep the herbs there for eight to twelve
hours. Do not wet or soak dried herbs. Fresh herbs should
be harvested as close as possible to the time you use them.
For best results, remember that fresh-cut herbs always last
longer when harvested from healthy, robust plants.

When we have our herb design workshops at our retail
store, I am always fascinated by the extremely gentle manner with which most attendees handle the herbs. This is, of
course, until they watch me dig in. Then they, too, begin to
cut and tie and tuck and glue, until to their amazement it
all comes together into a beautiful arrangement. Once they
get into the project, they realize how easy and how much
fun it is, and their anxieties about crumbling herbs and
shattered arrangements quickly disappear.

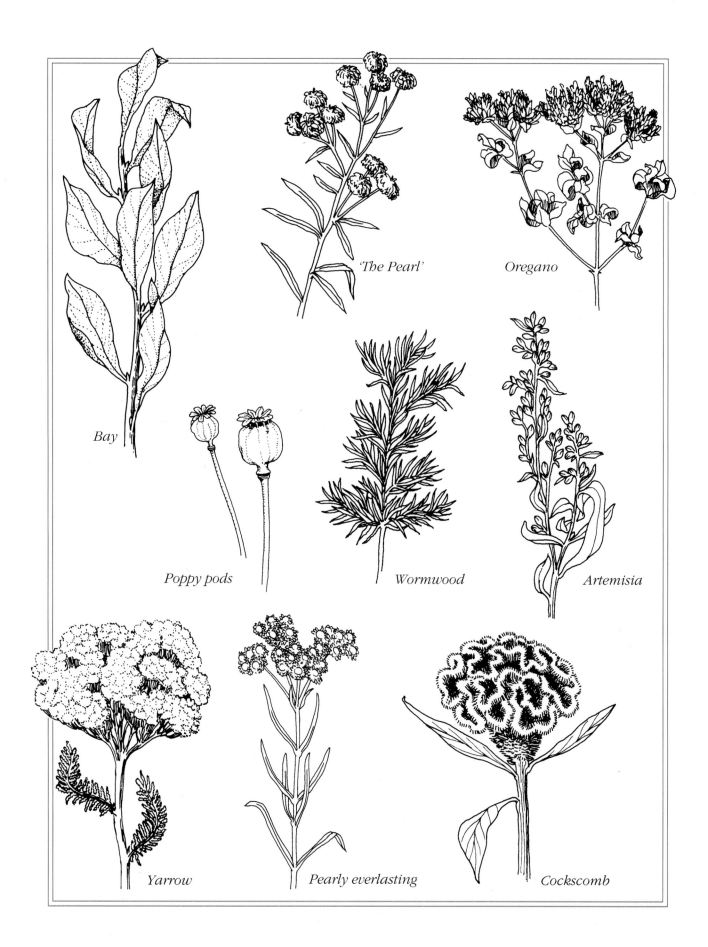

Bay

'The Pearl'

Oregano

Poppy pods

Wormwood

Artemisia

Yarrow

Pearly everlasting

Cockscomb

# SOME TIPS ON DRYING HERBS

*Rosemary*

Beginning with the first cutting of oregano in June every year, Marie hangs bunches of herbs to dry in our family room. On the north side of the house, out of direct sunlight, this room is our best location for drying herbs evenly and retaining their color and fragrance. By holiday time, the room is overflowing with dozens of different varieties of the herbs we grow. Before decorating the house, I spend one evening sorting and rearranging the bunches so that the colors and textures of the herbs are revealed in the most pleasing manner. This also gives me the chance to set aside the dried herbs I'll be using elsewhere as I begin my preparations for making the house a cheerful haven of the Christmas spirit for the Gilbertie family.

It's quite easy to dry herbs if you harvest them early in the morning right after the morning's moisture has left them. Clean off the bottom of the stems, wrap a rubber band around them, and hang them in a dark, dry place. "Dark and dry" are the key ingredients for really great-looking dried herbs. Bright light and moisture will break down their color and essential oils. A closet, back room, or dark attic will be perfect. If you just don't have such a place, try a large paper shopping bag, hung in a closet or pantry. Most herbs will dry within a week or two, and then you can store them away in cardboard boxes if you don't have enough hanging space.

*Eucalyptus*

# TECHNIQUES FOR SOME PROJECTS IN THIS BOOK

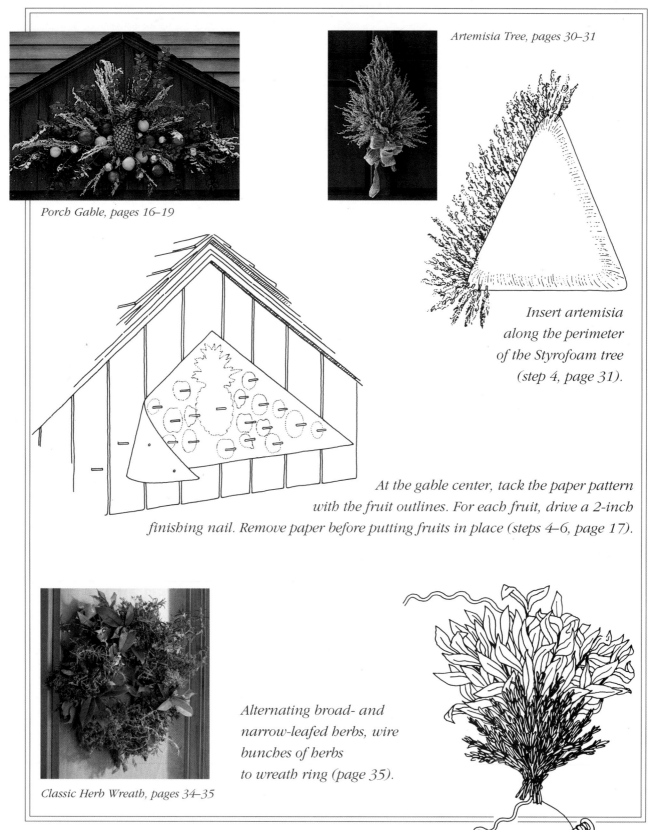

*Porch Gable, pages 16–19*

*Artemisia Tree, pages 30–31*

*Insert artemisia along the perimeter of the Styrofoam tree (step 4, page 31).*

*At the gable center, tack the paper pattern with the fruit outlines. For each fruit, drive a 2-inch finishing nail. Remove paper before putting fruits in place (steps 4–6, page 17).*

*Alternating broad- and narrow-leafed herbs, wire bunches of herbs to wreath ring (page 35).*

*Classic Herb Wreath, pages 34–35*

*Eucalyptus Wreath,*
*pages 32–33*

*Wire bunches of six to eight*
*6-inch eucalyptus stems*
*to wreath ring (step 4, page 33)*

*Alternate method for Eucalyptus or*
*Classic Herb Wreath: You may find it*
*easier to wire each bunch separately*
*before wiring it to the wreath ring.*

*Wreath with Teddy Bears, pages 38–39*

*Wire several bunches of birch branches with tips, and then*
*wire the bunches together to form a continuous 9-foot*
*length (steps 1–2, page 39).*

*The Peaceable Kingdom,
pages 86–89*

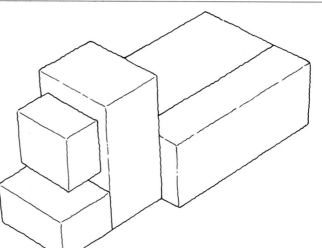

*Gluing floral foam together
as shown, carve animal shapes
with an ordinary kitchen knife. Because foam is very forgiving and because you
will be covering this mold with papier-mâché, you can push on it to refine the
shape, or glue on additional small pieces as needed.*

*Sconce, pages
102–103*

*Form 20-25 freeze-dried
cranberries into a 4-inch
semicircle, and glue
them together. Make
additional layers
of berries until the
piece is about 1 inch
high (step 1, page 103).*

*Chandelier, pages 104–106*

*Form 20-25 freeze-dried
cranberries into a circle,
about 1½ inches wide, and glue
the berries together (step 1, page 105)*

## SOURCES FOR PROJECT MATERIALS

*Most of the materials you will need to make the projects in this book are readily available. Here's where to look:*

| | |
|---|---|
| Fresh and dried herbs | *From the garden, hanging baskets and pots of herbs brought inside, herb farms, supermarkets* |
| Fruits | *Gourmet food markets, local orchards* |
| Dried materials, including corn, pomegranates, grapevines, vine wreaths, pepperberries, eucalyptus, evergreens, birch and willow branches, and bittersweet | *Craft stores, florist shops, garden centers, farm markets, wooded areas of friends and relatives* |
| Hot glue gun, Styrofoam, florist's wire, florist's pins, sheet moss, ribbons, paper bows, plastic candle holders | *Craft stores, florist shops, garden centers* |
| Paint, nails, plaster of paris, dowels, cardboard paint buckets, sand, hacksaw and blades | *Local hardware stores* |
| Tracing paper | *Art supply stores* |
| Millet, feed corn, bird seed | *Local Audubon shop, agricultural supplies stores, garden centers* |

CHAPTER 2

# Decorating the Outdoors

*H*erbs have a natural affinity for the outdoors. *After all, that's* where they are grown in profusion by every culture in the world. In combination with evergreens and other natural materials available during the holiday season, they become versatile decorations of welcome on doors, windows, porches, railings, pillars, lamp posts, and any other points of entry. I love to forage in the woods for boughs, pine cones, acorns, pieces of bark, and other found objects to incorporate into my exterior decorations. They give a unique, wild quality to my sprays and other arrangements. Once the outside of the house is dressed for Christmas, the magic of the holiday is truly in the air.

*⇐Holiday entry*

# Porch Columns and Gable

Because the front door is the main passage into the house, what better place to express the spirit of every season, none more special than Christmas. Our front porch welcomes friends and family in no uncertain terms during the Christmas holidays. You may not be able to judge a book by its cover, but you can safely surmise from the front door at the Gilberties that we're in the mood for an herbal holiday.

The pineapple, symbol of welcome, is the centerpiece in a display of herbs, gilded pomegranates, and other fruit that occupies the front porch gable. Holly, hemlock, and 'Silver King' artemisia encircle the side columns with their festive beauty. A bugling angel sounds the Christmas spirit from a vine wreath of baby's-breath and eucalyptus. Twin topiaries at the base of the steps serve as amiable sentries on guard duty for the season. On the door itself, a miniature tree of 'Silver King' artemisia provides a simple but elegant finishing touch.

Instructions for decorating the porch gable and columns follow; see pages 20–21 for the Apple and Pomegranate Topiary, pages 30–31 for the Two-Dimensional Artemisia Tree, and pages 40–41 for the Vine Wreath with Cherub.

## SIDE SPRAYS ATOP COLUMNS

1. Gild the pomegranates, following the directions in the box below.

2. To create a template, cut tracing paper to fit the space you are decorating, then place paper on a work table or other flat surface.

3. Place the fruits and gilded pomegranates on the tracing paper in a tree-shaped design. With a marking pen, outline the fruits and identify each shape.

4. Tack the paper to the desired location at the top of one of the porch columns.

5. For each fruit outlined, drive a 2-inch finishing nail into the gable or other surface; drive just far enough to secure it. (See drawing, page 10.)

6. When all the nails are in place, carefully remove the pattern.

7. Affix the fruits securely to the nails using your notes on the pattern as a guide.

## WHAT YOU WILL NEED

*24 pomegranates*

*18 small red apples*

*6 red pears*

*12 navel oranges*

*3 large red apples*

*3 large green apples*

*1 specimen pineapple*

*3 pounds green holly
(18–24 sprays per pound)*

*4 bunches 'Silver King'
artemisia (15–18 sprays
per bunch)*

*8 yards hemlock or pine
roping*

*shallow cardboard box*

*8-ounce can gold spray paint*

*2-foot x 6-foot roll tracing
paper*

*finishing nails*

> *2-inch: 50*
>
> *1-inch: 50*
>
> *2½-inch: 8*

## GILDING THE POMEGRANATES

*Place pomegranates in a shallow cardboard box. In a well-ventilated location, spray with gold spray paint until well covered. Let dry for two to three minutes, then shake the box to turn the fruit. Spray again. Repeat process until all fruit is completely gilded.*

8. For the opposite column, flop the pattern for symmetry, and repeat steps 5–7.

9. Wrap each column from top to bottom with hemlock or pine roping. Attach each rope at top and bottom and at intervals, where necessary, with 2-inch finishing nails.

10. Tuck branches of holly and artemisia behind the roping in a pleasing vertical pattern.

## Main Spray on Porch Gable

1. Cut tracing paper to fit space, then place paper on a work table or other flat surface.

2. To establish one half of your pattern, center the pineapple at one edge of paper and trace it with a marking pen.

3. Place other fruits in an attractive pattern (see photo) and outline them.

4. Placing the outline of the pineapple at the exact center, tack the paper to the gable.

5. Repeat steps 5–7 in "Side Sprays atop Columns."

6. Flop the pattern for symmetry, and complete decoration of the opposite half of the gable by again repeating steps 5–7. Use the 2½-inch nails to affix the pineapple.

7. Tuck branches of holly and artemisia in between fruit and pomegranates in a pleasing fan pattern. If necessary, fasten branches with 1-inch finishing nails.

*Main spray on porch gable*

# Apple and Pomegranate Topiary

A rustic topiary infused with holiday colors greets visitors with the humble bounty of a Connecticut apple orchard and the elegant indulgence of gilded pomegranates. Strands of 'Silver King' artemisia and bay and holly leaves, woven into the globe of the topiary, lend graceful notes of gray and green, and a natural paper bow adds a sophisticated flourish.

    This topiary is over three feet high, so it can stand alone or as one of a pair in an entry of any size, and it is compatible with just about any style of residential architecture. It is most congenial in a country setting, I think, but it has enough formality to suit a Park Avenue apartment. It could be used inside the house, too, where it would be spectacular on a table in the hall or dining room, or in a prominent window.

To me, topiary is the gardener's ultimate art form, and this sculpture in red, green, and gold is a festive reminder, in the dead of winter, of the glory of more fruitful seasons.

## BUILDING THE TOPIARY

1. Gild the pomegranates (see box, page 17).

2. Place the dowel in the center of the bucket, and fill to three-quarters with sand.

3. Mix plaster of paris. Pour over sand to fill bucket to top. Allow two days to dry.

4. Impale the Styrofoam ball securely on top of the dowel.

5. Wrap dowel with sheet moss, tying it in place with florist's wire as you go.

6. Wind grapevine over the sheet moss, securing it at the top and bottom with florist's wire.

7. Wrap the Styrofoam ball with sheet moss. Secure it with florist's pins or plasterboard nails.

8. Insert finishing nails, head first, into twelve apples and twelve gilded pomegranates. For the pomegranates, puncture the entry holes first with the sharp end of the nail, then insert the head of the nail into the opening.

9. Pin apples and pomegranates into the ball, leaving space between them.

10. Insert artemisia stems and bay leaf or holly stems into the ball to fill the spaces between the fruit.

11. Place the finished topiary in the basket. Use remaining apples to fill in around the top of the basket.

12. Tie a bow onto the dowel beneath the topiary head.

### WHAT YOU WILL NEED

*12 dried pomegranates*

*1 pound sheet moss*

*1 woody grapevine, 4 feet long*

*24 small red apples*

*1 bunch 'Silver King' artemisia (20 stems), or 1 pound green holly, cut into 4-inch lengths*

*1 bunch bay (20 stems), cut into 4-inch lengths*

*shallow cardboard box*

*8-ounce can gold spray paint*

*3-foot dowel, ¾ inch in diameter*

*½ of 25-pound bag of sand*

*5-pound bag plaster of paris*

*basket (peck size)*

*cardboard paint bucket (hardware-store variety) to fit inside basket*

*8-inch Styrofoam ball*

*1 standard roll 24-gauge florist's wire*

*36 florist's pins, or 1½-inch plasterboard nails*

*24 finishing nails (2½-inch)*

*large natural paper bow*

*Detail of pine cone*

# A Winter Wildlife Arbor

We built the grape arbor behind our garden as a summer refuge for the family. It's a great place to sit out of the sun with a glass of iced mint tea and a good book. The vines are usually completely leafed out by the middle of May, and grapes are ready to pick in mid-September. I planted the same purple Concord variety my grandfather liked to grow. This versatile grape can be eaten out of hand or used for making delicious jams, jellies, and juices. Concords grow quickly, and in only two years the productive vines — one measuring twenty feet across — covered our large arbor.

In winter, the arbor, bleak and empty, is another story. When the holiday season rolls around, however, I transform it into a kind of wildlife refuge that's both festive and functional. Garden gates, an attractive fence or trellis, a porch or carport could be decorated in a similar fashion. The garlands of corn, millet, and apples attract squirrels, whitetail deer, and wild turkeys. Because our main interest is in feeding the birds, however, I hang feeders full of seed from the main beams of the arbor and attach large pine cones (sugar pine cones are best, if you can get them) laden with peanut butter and sunflower seeds to the poles. Cardinals, finches, chickadees, titmice, grosbeaks, and many other varieties flock to the arbor daily, a warming sight that never loses its spectator appeal.

## DECORATING AN ARBOR

1. Pour sunflower seed into a shallow cardboard carton. Using a flat knife, spread peanut butter into the crevices of the pine cones. Then, roll each pine cone in the seed, using pressure to secure the seed in the peanut butter.

2. Tack nails on the tops of the vertical poles of the arbor. Use florist's wire to attach the pine cones to the nails.

3. With the saw or knife, split cobs of corn in thirds (2–3 inches long).

4. Tie narrow ribbon or twine to the poles in garland fashion, then tack finishing nails to the poles at 6–8-inch intervals, using the garland as your guide.

5. Impale the corn sections (through core) and whole apples onto the nails in an alternating pattern.

6. Weave millet on the garlands between the corn and apples.

7. Make up large bows of the wide ribbon, and tie them to the posts above the pine cones with florist's wire.

### WHAT YOU WILL NEED

*10 pounds sunflower seed*

*1 quart jar smooth peanut butter*

*six 12–15-inch sugar pine cones (or largest cones available)*

*1 bushel husked feed corn on the cob*

*1 bushel Macoun, McIntosh, or Red Delicious apples*

*2 dozen millet sprays*

*shallow cardboard carton*

*100 finishing nails (2½-inch)*

*1 standard roll 24-gauge florist's wire*

*hacksaw or heavy kitchen knife with serrated blade*

*1 bolt narrow ribbon or twine (25 yards)*

*1 bolt 4-inch-wide red exterior ribbon (25 yards)*

CHAPTER 3

# Wreaths, Sprays, and Swags

*H*erbs impart a special character to traditional Christmas wreaths, as well as more formal swags and garlands. The herb kingdom offers literally thousands of different colors and textures to use for making decorations. No two wreaths or swags are the same in our house, thanks to this variety. Sages, lavenders, thymes, artemisias, lamb's-ears, and many other herbs also dry beautifully, so arrangements remain fresh looking throughout the holidays. From a common kitchen garden of herbs, one can fashion an uncommonly attractive wreath or a pretty swag for a mirror or mantel.

# RUSTIC SPRAY OF HERBS AND GREENS

Sometimes we forget how much beauty exists in nature, even during the barren winter months of a northern climate. I gathered the material used in this outsized spray —it measures about four feet long—on a short walk through the woods near our home.

The real inspiration for the spray came from an abandoned wasps' nest I found. I saw its papery natural form as a wonder of insect architecture. To call attention to it, I made it the centerpiece of a very rustic assemblage of boughs and branches. My barn door was the perfect place to hang it, but a similar spray would look attractive on a garage door or bleak exterior wall.

Improvisation is the key with a piece like this. Not everyone will stumble on an abandoned wasps' nest. The fun is to stalk the world of nature for whatever catches your eye, then put the wild elements together in pleasing fashion, using whatever evergreens are available in your area.

## CREATING A SPRAY

1. On a floor in a basement, garage, or barn, arrange the boughs of evergreens in a pleasing fashion, then wrap stem ends tightly with florist's wire to fasten them securely together. Add birch branches, tying them tightly to the bough spray in a desirable pattern.

2. Attach the bow so it covers the woody stems, and tie in several handfuls of mountain mint or oregano.

3. Peel the shell off the nest, and carefully tie the shell directly below bow.

4. Separate the layers of the nest with a flat knife and tie them to the branches.

5. Tie sprigs of mountain mint or oregano to other branches as needed.

### WHAT YOU WILL NEED

*8–10 boughs of white pine, cedar, and juniper (36–40 inches long)*

*four 1-inch-diameter birch branches*

*12–15 stems mountain mint or oregano*

*abandoned wasps' nest (make certain the nest is no longer in use)*

*1 standard roll 18- or 22-gauge florist's wire*

*large red paper bow*

# FEED-THE-BIRDS WREATH

This is a simple wreath for a sublime purpose—to feed the birds that come to our backyard in the winter. The vine wreath itself is a grizzled veteran of many years. We rehabilitate it for the holidays every year by adding willow and birch tips, bittersweet, and wild grapevines gathered from the woods.

The attraction for the birds is all the grains I incorporate into the wreath. Wheat, barley, and millet, along with sunflower heads (from the miniature variety 'Big Smile'), are the main course. Even though the wreath is hung on the side of the house next to our busy back door, the birds begin to feed on it almost immediately, and we often replace the grains several times a season.

One year, it received the ultimate accolade from the birds—a pair of house finches built a nest in it in the spring.

## THE WREATH

1. Tuck the willow and birch tips and the bittersweet vine into the grapevine base in a loose pattern. Secure with glue gun.

2. Tie small bunches (six to eight pieces) of barley and wheat to the wreath with florist's wire.

3. Weave in millet sprays.

4. Affix sunflower heads with glue gun.

5. Fasten the large paper bow at the top with florist's wire.

6. Carefully tuck additional barley and wheat in any empty spaces between branches.

7. Replenish bird feed as needed.

## WHAT YOU WILL NEED

*40–50 willow branch tips (12–15 inches long)*

*40–50 birch branch tips (12–15 inches long)*

*10 bittersweet vines (24 inches long)*

*30-inch preformed grapevine wreath*

*1 bunch barley (50 stems)*

*1 bunch wheat (50 stems)*

*12 sprays millet*

*12 mini-sunflower heads*

*hot glue gun and glue sticks*

*fifteen 18-inch lengths 24-gauge florist's wire*

*large paper bow*

# Two-Dimensional Artemisia Tree

This simple Christmas tree of 'Silver King' artemisia creates a stunning effect on a dark painted or wood-grain sur–face, where most green herbs would not show up. It looks like a tiny spruce tree just after a fresh snowfall. At our house, the front door is the perfect setting for such an arrangement.

## Making the Tree

1. With a sharp blade or hacksaw, cut a triangular tree form, 12 inches high and 8 inches wide at base out of Styrofoam.

2. Use the saw to round off the sharp edges of the tree form on the front side.

3. Form a hanger by tying twine securely around the middle of the form and making a loop on the back side. Pull the twine tightly so that it secures itself slightly into the Styrofoam. Be careful not to pull too hard, or you may cut through the Styrofoam.

4. Insert 4-inch lengths of artemisia along the perimeter of the tree. Next, fill in the tree from the outside to the center and from the top to the bottom, reserving the 2-inch lengths for the base area. (See drawing, page 10.)

5. Use a glue gun to affix the chili peppers to the tree in an attractive pattern.

6. Tie the bow at the base of the tree with florist's wire.

## What You Will Need

*2 bunches 'Silver King' artemisia (80 stems), 2- to 4-inch lengths*

*36 red dried chili peppers*

*1 block 2-inch x 8-inch x 12-inch Styrofoam*

*18-inch length twine*

*hot glue gun and glue sticks*

*paper bow*

*two 18-inch lengths 24-gauge florist's wire*

# EUCALYPTUS WREATH

Eucalyptus is available in astonishing variety—upwards of 500 species—but my favorite for making wreaths and other herbal decorations is a variety called 'Spiral', so-called because of its unique leaf pattern and coloration. A wreath made from 'Spiral' eucalyptus has a weathered patina and a cool, sculptural quality that remind me of ancient monuments on forgotten squares in Italy. Ornamented with gilded pomegranates and sprigs of colorful pepperberries, a eucalyptus wreath offers an interesting, more formal contrast to softer, conventional Christmas wreaths. The pleasant, spicy fragrance of the herb itself, a medicinal plant of long standing, complements the aromas of the traditional Christmas herbs rosemary and artemisia, which we use profusely in other decorations.

We always hang our eucalyptus wreath in the living room, the most formal room in our house, but it really could be displayed anywhere, even on a front door.

## THE WREATH

1. Spray dried pomegranates with gold paint (see box on page 17).

2. Cut the eucalyptus stems into 6-inch lengths. Reserve about a dozen of the most attractive tip ends.

3. Tie the reserved tip ends together with a 12-inch length of florist's wire, to make a single bunch. Cover the wire with decorative ribbon and set the bunch aside.

4. Gather six to eight 6-inch eucalyptus stems, place them on the wire ring, and secure firmly with florist's wire. If you find it difficult to handle the stems in this way, you can tie them into bundles before wiring them to the ring. (See drawings, page 11.)

5. Repeat this process, overlapping stem ends with each subsequent bunch, until the wire ring is completely covered.

6. If there are any gaps in the wreath, fill in with single stems attached with hot glue.

7. Place pomegranates around the wreath at desired intervals, and attach them by applying hot glue to the stem end of the fruit. Hold firmly in place until secure.

8. Glue pepperberry sprigs in place around each pome-granate.

9. With florist's wire, attach the bunch of tip ends to the reverse side of wreath so that the eucalyptus hangs from the base of the wreath. Glue the other end of the decorative ribbon to the top reverse side of wreath.

### WHAT YOU WILL NEED

*6 dried pomegranates*

*1½ pounds 'Spiral' eucalyptus (24 stems)*

*6 sprigs pepperberries*

*shallow cardboard box*

*8-ounce can gold spray paint*

*1 standard roll 24-gauge florist's wire*

*18 inches of 1-inch-wide decorative ribbon*

*10-inch single-wire steel wreath ring*

*hot glue gun and glue sticks*

# CLASSIC HERB WREATH

An herbal wreath is one of the most popular Christmas decorations for the home. It offers the same useful and domesticated beauty that the herb garden itself does. It evokes values we associate with farm and pioneer families. I make a variety of herbal wreaths for different locations around our house, sometimes adding small fruits, berries, and pine cones for different effects.

Of our fall workshops, the wreath workshops are invariably the ones that draw the greatest crowds. People like to make these wreaths for their own homes as well as for gifts. One year, a student who took the class for the first time made a beautiful wreath, which she planned to give to a friend for Christmas. When she came to take the class again a year later, however, she confessed that she had made the mistake of placing it in the middle of her dining room table when she got home and that the wreath was still there, her permanent centerpiece.

In fact, an herbal wreath will last a year or more, especially if you mist it with water from time to time, after it has dried thoroughly, to keep it fresh looking.

Use florist's wire to tie the bunches securely (but not so firmly that the wire cuts into the stems) to the wreath frame in the above order, alternating broad- and narrow-leafed herbs. Repeat the sequence three times to fill out the wreath. If this technique is difficult to manage, you may wire the bunches together before wiring them to the wreath frame. (See drawings, pages 10–11.)

## WHAT YOU WILL NEED

*three bunches (36–45 stems) each:*

>*oregano*
>
>*mountain mint*
>
>*thyme*
>
>*purple sage*
>
>*chili peppers*
>
>*bay*
>
>*rosemary*

*12-inch single-wire steel wreath frame*

*1 standard roll 26-gauge florist's wire*

**Note:** *Most right-handed persons work clockwise, starting from the 12 o'clock position at the top of the frame; left-handers generally go the other way. The important thing is to make sure the bunches are evenly distributed throughout to give the wreath uniform body.*

# WREATH WITH TEDDY BEARS

My oldest son, Sal, was the inspiration for this wreath, at
least indirectly. In the attic one day, I came upon the tiny
teddy bear that used to be his favorite companion, night
and day. It reminded me of all the times I'd sung "The
Teddy Bears' Picnic" to Sal and later to our other children
when they were small, and I decided to make a wreath as
a kind of Christmas tribute to those memories.

Birch and willow are the basic building materials, because of their whimsical, woodsy associations. I deliberately shaped the wreath into an oval to make room for Sal's bear and two friends. This informal, frolicsome wreath is most at home in the family room or gathering room.

Treasured teddy bears, dolls, and other toys often have as much emotional value for families as more traditional holiday keepsakes. It's fun to find a place of honor for them once again during the Christmas season. Don't be surprised if something warm and wonderful turns up in one of the trunks in your attic, too.

## MAKING THE WREATH

1. Tie the base ends of the birch branches together to form bunches about 12 inches wide at the tips.

2. Overlap one bunch on another, with stems running in the same direction, and tie the two bunches together firmly with florist's wire. Add the remaining bunches, one by one, in the same way to form one continuous 9-foot length. Bend this length into a circle and tie the ends together. (See drawing, page 11.)

3. Tie willow branches to the birch wreath in an overlapping pattern, while shaping the entire wreath into an oval form. This shaping process sometimes requires tying heavier branches to the back side in order to achieve your desired form.

4. With hot glue gun, affix stems of white pearl yarrow in a pleasing pattern throughout upper section of wreath.

5. Glue mountain mint and oregano to the base, hiding any gaps in wreath.

6. Glue the red globe amaranth to the wreath as desired.

7. Weave gingham ribbon into the wreath as shown.

8. Hang the wreath in place, and position the teddy bears.

## WHAT YOU WILL NEED

*15–20 birch branches with tips (3–4 feet long)*

*6 willow branches with tips (3–4 feet long)*

*2 bunches dried white pearl yarrow,* Achillea *'The Pearl' (40–50 stems)*

*1 bunch dried mountain mint (20 stems)*

*1 bunch dried oregano (20 stems)*

*9 bunches dried red globe amaranth,* Gomphrena *(108 stems)*

*1 standard roll 22-gauge florist's wire*

*hot glue gun and glue sticks*

*2 yards decorative gingham ribbon*

*3 small teddy bears (or dolls)*

## Vine Wreath with Cherub

When I first came upon a charming cherub figure a few years ago, I knew I wanted to use it somewhere near our front entrance for the holidays. This trumpeting angel seemed appropriate for two reasons. It conveyed a sense of jubilant welcome, and it evoked the "good news" associated with the holiday ever since the first Christmas.

I decided to create a rustic counterpoint to the classic lines of the sculpture by framing it in an irregular vine wreath to which I added touches of wildness in the form of birch tips. The verdigris-colored eucalyptus, 'Silver King' artemisia, and pretty reds of the pepperberries add brightness as well as texture. Dried baby's-breath, roses, and peonies reflect the essential sweetness of the central image of the cherub.

## VINE WREATH

1. Tuck birch tips into the vine wreath in an even pattern throughout. Glue them where necessary.

2. Add eucalyptus, artemisia, and pepperberries, placing them symmetrically and gluing them as necessary.

3. Carefully place and glue the dried roses and peonies in a pleasing pattern.

4. Break off small clusters of dried baby's-breath and then tuck into place around the lower half of the wreath to fill in any empty spaces.

5. Hang the wreath, and set the cherub in place.

### WHAT YOU WILL NEED

*1 bunch birch branch tips (fifty 12-inch pieces)*

*18-inch-diameter preformed vine wreath*

*9 stems 'Spiral' eucalyptus*

*6 stems 'Silver King' artemisia*

*12 sprigs red pepperberries*

*6 dried roses*

*6 dried peonies*

*½ bunch dried baby's-breath (30 short clusters)*

*hot glue gun and glue sticks*

*cherub figure*

# Angel's Head Swag

One of the first decorations I put up for the Christmas season is the vine swag featuring an angelic painted porcelain head I found in an antique shop years ago. We place it over the arched doorway in our dining room. It makes an elegant touch and, with its dried roses, a suggestion of romance.

I forage in the woods for the vines for this piece, because I find that wild grapes produce twistier vines than their domestic counterparts, and these less regular forms are more effective in this type of swag design.

A doll's head or any fetching likeness could be substituted for the tiny porcelain bust to achieve the same effect (see title page). Any combination of herbs, flowers, and antiques is unfailingly romantic.

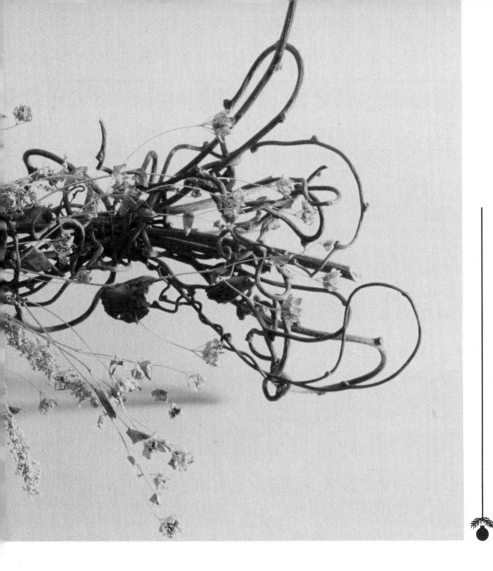

## WHAT YOU WILL NEED

*8–10 branches fresh-cut twisted grapevine ends (24–36 inches long)*

*12 stems mountain mint*

*3 stems 'Silver King' artemisia*

*12 dried red roses*

*ten 18-inch lengths 24-gauge florist's wire*

*ceramic figure, or similar centerpiece*

*24-inch length clear fishing line*

*hot glue gun and glue sticks*

## CREATING THE SWAG

1. Shape the freshly cut grapevine into a swag measuring 18 to 24 inches. Use florist's wire to secure.

2. Tie the ceramic figure to the swag with clear fishing line.

3. Using glue gun, affix mountain mint, artemisia, and roses in between vines to fill in around figure.

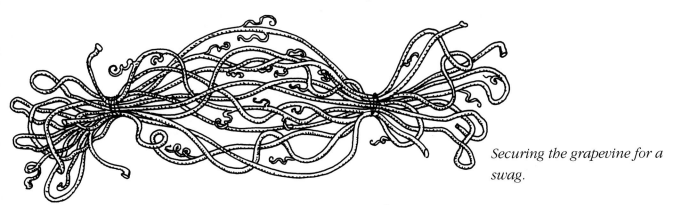

*Securing the grapevine for a swag.*

# Christmas Trees

*I* *can't remember a year when the Gilbertie family*
celebrated Christmas with only one Christmas tree. The
form is so powerful and enticing that I like to have several
in different sizes and styles. Herbs add an element of the
unexpected to this traditional centerpiece of the holiday.
Even a diminutive artificial tree assumes a perky impor-
tance with the addition of a pleasing variety of dried herbs.
When there are small children in the family, the tree
should be playful and ablaze with color. A more sedate
and elegant tree fits perfectly in a formal room in the
house. If you have glass ornaments and other decorations
handed down over generations, even if they are a bit worn
around the edges, so much the better.

# Candy Cane and Toy Tree

The peppermint candy canes on the Christmas tree that I decorate especially for the children serve an important purpose at our house during the holidays—as pacifiers. I put several dozen canes on the tree, left in their original cellophane wrapping, along with a sprig of variegated lemon balm tied onto each cane with a small red bow.

When our kids or visiting children become tired, cranky, or bored (as usually happens when the adults sit down after lunch or dinner for a cup of coffee), Marie pours them a cup of warm water and invites them to "have tea" with us. Each child picks out his or her own candy cane from the tree, drops the lemon balm in the water, unwraps the cane, and stirs the infusion with the candy. The lemon balm gives the water a tealike flavor, and the peppermint adds the sweetness kids enjoy.

The ornaments we've collected over the years for this tree are likenesses of animals, cars, drums, and other toys — images that children respond to. Similarly, under the tree I always place a few cherished old toys and stuffed animals to remind us all of the timelessness of Christmas.

## Decorating the Tree

1. Make up 36 small red bows for the candy canes. Use florist's wire to tie them securely.

2. Place a stem of lemon balm or mint on each candy cane. Use the florist's wire on each red bow to fasten it to the candy.

3. Set up the tree, and string the lights.

4. Decorate with candy canes and ornaments.

5. Tie ribbons to the peak of the tree, and trail them down to the base.

6. Place the angel on the top of the tree.

## What You Will Need

*36 small candy canes (6–8 inch)*

*36 small stems of lemon balm with leaves*

*6-foot Douglas fir or other soft-needled evergreen tree*

*1 roll ½-inch-wide red ribbon (25 yards)*

*thirty-six 9-inch lengths 26-gauge florist's wire*

*tree stand*

*2 strands tiny white Christmas lights*

*100 assorted ornaments*

*1 roll 1-inch-wide candy-cane-striped ribbons (25 yards)*

*1 roll 1-inch-wide gingham ribbon (25 yards)*

*antique angel doll, or other appropriate figure, for top of tree*

# GARDENER'S CHRISTMAS TREE

This tree is perfect for a keeping room or family den—any informal space in the house where the family likes to gather. Trimmed with fruits, vegetables, herbs, and grains, the tree is the gardener's expression of Christmas, a thankful tribute to the harvest. When lights are added to the tree, the fresh orange slices acquire a wonderful translucence, as does the star fashioned from cornhusks atop the tree.

Glass ornaments made in the likeness of the bounty from the garden add traditional gleam and glitter to the tree. Antique ornaments, which are hard to come by and often expensive, are good things to scout for throughout the year at flea markets, garage sales, or antique stores. Newly made ornaments in familiar fruit and vegetable shapes are available in some stores and gardening catalogs.

We always set up the gardener's tree in the family room where "Pepino" pays his annual Christmas Eve visit to all the children in our extended family. Pepino is a Gilbertie family tradition that I started some years ago. The hired local actor, dressed as Santa's head elf, shows up the night before Christmas to give presents to boys and girls who've shown themselves to be worthy in special ways during the year. If Gretchen walked the dog for a sick neighbor, or Michael helped his mother with the Christmas baking, then Pepino calls attention to their good deeds and rewards them with a stick of candy or a wind-up toy.

After all the kids have been singled out (we manage to uncover at least one streak of good behavior in each child every year), Pepino tells the children they had better take their parents home now that Christmas is almost upon us. We never planned it this way, but this tactic clears out the house immediately, leaving Marie and me alone to complete our holiday preparations.

## WHAT YOU WILL NEED

*6-foot Douglas fir (or other soft-needled evergreen) tree*

*6 navel oranges*

*3 dozen dried red chili peppers*

*2 dozen stems artemisia*

*2 dozen stems, wheat, barley, or rye*

*1 dozen miniature strawberry corn*

*6 ears husked feed corn*

*1 dozen Lady apples with stems*

*2 dozen walnuts (in the shell)*

*tree stand*

*2 strands of tiny white Christmas tree lights*

*1 standard roll 26-gauge florist's wire*

*hot glue gun and glue sticks*

*hacksaw or heavy kitchen knife with serrated blade*

*drill with 1/64-inch bit*

*6-inch square of sturdy cardboard*

*4 dozen ornament hangers*

*2 dozen antique glass ornaments*

*2 dozen fruit and vegetable ornaments*

## DECORATING THE TREE

1. Set up the tree, and string the lights.

2. Slice the oranges in ¼-inch rounds, discarding the heels.

3. Cut florist's wire into 4-inch lengths and bend to form s-shaped hooks. Use these to hang approximately 30 orange slices so they are evenly distributed. Locate each in front of a light.

4. Cluster two or three red chili peppers with a stem of artemisia, and use a glue gun to affix the clusters to branches. Reserve about ten peppers for the star in step 10.

5. Use florist's wire to tie stems of wheat to the outer tips of branches.

6. Remove the husks from the miniature corn. Reserve the husks and use florist's wire to hang the corn on the tree.

7. With the saw or knife, cut the feed-corn cobs into 2-inch lengths. Drill holes through the center of each round, and use florist's wire to suspend the corn from the tree.

**8.** Tightly wrap florist's wire around stems and hang the apples.

**9.** Drill a hole through each walnut; use florist's wire to hang them.

**10.** To make the star, assemble the reserved cornhusks and about ten red chili peppers. Cut a 4-inch round out of sturdy cardboard. Glue a single layer of cornhusks to the cardboard. Place the husks with their tips pointing outward, approximately eight husks to the layer. Add two additional layers, arranging the husks so that the circumference of the star has numerous points. Then, glue a layer of about eight peppers to the center of the star in a circular pattern, with the tips of the peppers pointing outward. Attach the star to the peak of the tree with florist's wire.

**11.** Hang the glass ornaments.

*Treetop cornhusk and chili pepper star*

# Ribbons-and-Roses Tree

We like to trim the tree in our living room with our most elegant decorations. The traditional look of the tree is suitable for this, the most formal room in our house. The starburst arrangement of eucalyptus, baby's-breath, and dried red roses at the treetop forms a majestic floral crown to the holiday creation. This is the tree where Marie and I find our gifts to each other on Christmas morning.

## Making the Starburst Arrangement

1. Set up the tree, and string the lights.

2. Tie the eight lengths of eucalyptus together at the stem ends with florist's wire.

3. Carefully spread apart the eucalyptus, and affix one dozen dried red roses around the outside of the bouquet in a pleasing pattern. Tie the stems at the base with florist's wire.

*Treetop roses and eucalyptus spray*

## What You Will Need

*6-foot Douglas fir (or other soft-needled evergreen) tree*

*eight 10-inch lengths 'Spiral' eucalyptus tips*

*12 stems dried red roses*

*115–120 small clusters dried baby's-breath*

*6 dozen dried yellow roses*

*6 dozen dried red or pink roses*

*tree stand*

*3 strands white Christmas lights*

*fifty 18-inch lengths 26-gauge florist's wire*

*1 roll 1½-inch-wide cranberry satin ribbon (25 yards)*

*1 roll ½-inch-wide gold braided ribbon (25 yards)*

*hot glue gun and glue sticks*

*100 assorted glass ball ornaments*

4. Insert dried baby's-breath uniformly throughout to fill empty spaces. (Use glue gun if baby's-breath will not stay in place.) Use fifteen to twenty of the clusters of baby's-breath for this purpose; the remainder will be used to create the bouquets described below.

5. Form one large cranberry ribbon bow, with eight 6-inch loops and six 24-inch tails.

6. Cut six 24-inch lengths of gold braided ribbon, and glue the ends to the base of cranberry ribbon bow so that the gold ribbon trails on tails of the cranberry.

7. Use florist's wire to affix the bow and bouquet to the peak of the tree, allowing the tails of the bow to flow uniformly down all sides. Handle this fragile arrangement with care while securing it into position. You will need help with this, especially while on the ladder.

## BOUQUETS AND RIBBONS

1. Make up four dozen 4–5 inch diameter bouquets, each consisting of three red or yellow roses and two clusters of baby's-breath. Use florist's wire to secure.

2. Trim the tree with cranberry and gold-braided ribbons in garland fashion, weaving the two ribbons together as you go.

3. Place bouquets uniformly throughout the tree, securing with florist's wire as needed.

4. Hang ornaments.

# TABLETOP TREES WITH POTPOURRI

A diminutive tabletop tree is a wonderful gift for a person living in a small space, but it also finds a welcome perch in the largest of houses, in a window, on a bookshelf or mantel, or on an otherwise-forgotten small table.

I like the way these very simple decorations breathe life and color into an inexpensive product. Without pretending to be a real tree, the creation achieves a natural beauty, anyway. The effect comes from the dried herbs used to embellish the form — white pearl yarrow at the base, red globe amaranth at the tips, and mountain mint interspersed among the branches.

As a companion to each tree, we make up a bowl of potpourri from the same natural ingredients, picking up the colors, scents, and sentiment of the tree.

*Red globe amaranth*

## YARROW AND GLOBE AMARANTH TREE

1. Wrap the base of the tree in burlap, and tie with twine.

2. Secure stems of white pearl yarrow among branches throughout tree with glue gun.

3. Using the glue gun, affix amaranth globes to tips of branches on all sides.

4. Fill remaining spaces with sprigs of mountain mint or oregano.

5. **To make the potpourri,** combine ½ cup each of globe amaranth, pieces of yarrow, and mountain mint leaves with the pine cones in a plastic bag. Add ⅛ ounce of the fragrant oil, and toss gently. Allow to sit for 24 hours. Pour mixture into a favorite small antique bowl.

## WHAT YOU WILL NEED

*artificial tree, 18–20 inches high*

*1 bunch white pearl yarrow, Achillea 'The Pearl' (20 stems)*

*50–60 red globe amaranth flowers (Gomphrena)*

*½ bunch mountain mint or oregano (10 stems)*

*1 cup miniature pine cones*

*¼ ounce balsam or pine fragrant oil (such as Balsam Eve)*

*18-inch square of burlap*

*12-inch length of twine*

*hot glue gun and glue sticks*

# Roses, Amaranth, and Statice Tree

On a table in the den, Marie keeps a large, old decorative bowl, where she collects small dried flowers all year — from the gardens, as well as from gift bouquets she receives. Pinks, whites, lavenders, and mauves are her favorites. By November, the bowl is overflowering with her own special blend of unfragranced potpourri. It makes for great pickin's in creating a matching table tree for the den.  For fragrance, we add a seasonal fragrant oil, such as Balsam Eve or Cranberry Cinnamon.

1. Mix the plaster of paris, and pour it into the clay pot until the pot is filled to the top.

2. Place the stem of the tree into the center of the pot, and then set aside to dry for 24 hours.

3. Glue the statice and globe amaranth flowers to the tips of the branches, distributing them evenly throughout the tree.

4. Tuck the curry pieces between the flowers, using a glue gun if necessary.

5. Glue the lamb's-ears flowers and roses in the remaining spaces.

6. Fill in with dried baby's-breath and Spanish moss.

## What You Will Need

*artificial tree, 15–18 inches high*

*12 single pieces of pink dried statice flowers*

*12 single pieces of purple dried statice flowers*

*24–36 pink globe amaranth flowers (Gomphrena)*

*twelve 4-inch pieces of dried curry plant*

*4 lamb's-ears flowers, cut into 1-inch pieces*

*12 dried red rose heads*

*24 short clusters of dried baby's-breath*

*handful of Spanish moss*

*1 cup dried white rose, or other dried flower, petals*

*¼ ounce fragrant oil — balsam (such as Balsam Eve), pine, or cranberry (such as Cranberry Cinnamon)*

*1 pound plaster of paris*

*4- or 5-inch clay pot (preferably old and moss covered)*

*hot glue gun and glue sticks*

# CHAPTER 5

# Decorations for Holiday Feasts

*T*he Christmas kitchen at our house draws on the flavors of herbs in both traditional and surprising ways, enhancing virtually all the dishes we serve, from appetizers to desserts. Many of the beverages we offer our guests, most notably our herbal teas, are flavored with herbs. In addition to every special holiday event we host, Marie and I like to add a decorative herbal note in the form of bouquets, centerpieces, and other arrangements. Herbs are inextricably linked with food and celebration during the holiday, and we would not have it any other way.

⇐ *Christmas Eve wreath, with roses and daisies in center*

# ADVENT WREATH

The first day of Advent, four Sundays before December 25, marks the beginning of the Christmas season. Traditionally, we bring an Advent wreath into the house at that time and hang our Advent calendar to serve as a daily reminder of the coming feast and to encourage anticipation as well as thankful contemplation of the holiday.

Never far from our thoughts, our Advent wreath serves as the centerpiece for our evening meals and Sunday dinners in the weeks leading up to Christmas. It's the first holiday decoration I make for the family, and I put as much Christmas spirit and hope into the making of it as I do time.

I vary the combination of evergreens and herbs, depending on what in my garden looks best or offers the most interesting contrast at the time I put the wreath together. Periodic spritzing keeps the wreath looking and smelling fresh. For Christmas week, I sometimes use fresh sprigs of herbs to replace the rosemary, sage, and thyme, if they've lost their perkiness. Lamb's-ears surround the base of each of the four candles, which are in the traditional colors of purple and, for rejoicing, pink.

## THE WREATH

1. Place the Styrofoam ring in the plastic container, then line the inside circle of the ring with pine cones gluing them in place with the hot glue gun.

2. Insert the candleholders at regular intervals in the ring.

3. Cover the Styrofoam base with cedar. Use florist's pins to anchor the cedar.

4. Insert sprigs of boxwood and holly into the Styrofoam in a uniform pattern.

5. Insert lamb's-ears around the base of each candle.

6. Arrange herb bunches in a pleasing pattern between the holly and boxwood, filling all empty spaces.

7. Insert the candles.

## WHAT YOU WILL NEED

*9 assorted small pinecones*

*three 12–15-inch branches of cedar*

*three 12–15-inch branches of boxwood*

*three 12–15-inch branches of holly*

*assorted small bunches, 8–10 stems each, of fresh rosemary, golden thyme, bay, lamb's-ears, purple sage, and tricolor sage (santolina, curry plant, and golden sage are suitable substitutes)*

*12-inch Styrofoam ring*

*18-inch shallow plastic container (recycle one from a catering deli or pastry shop)*

*hot glue gun and glue sticks*

*36 florist's pins*

*4 plastic candleholders*

*1 pink and 3 purple candles*

# $\mathcal{A}$ Christmas Kitchen

Several times during the holidays, usually when it's frosty outside, we make up a batch of mulled apple cider and leave it steaming on the kitchen counter for whoever stops by. With cinnamon sticks, star anise, allspice, and cloves floating in the brew, the bowl of cider and its delicious aroma is an inviting presence, as is the home-made gingerbread farmhouse created by my cousin Maria. No one is allowed to nibble on the farmhouse until Christmas Day, and then the rule is to eat the silo and the barnyard and figures first and start on the house from the back.

Most kitchens are busy year-round, but during the holiday season they are like Grand Central Station. Because it is so busy, our kitchen is not an easy place to decorate—the last thing the chef and sous-chef need is pretty but extraneous clutter. On the other hand, I've always believed that Santa's elves ought to enjoy Christmas as much as the people the elves are working so hard for. That's why I make a special effort to enliven the workplace with Christmas cheer and sparkle.

A kitchen garland is easy to fashion and adds a festive atmosphere to the room without interfering with holiday baking. The materials listed here are enough for one six-foot length.

## What You Will Need

*3 dried pomegranates*

*1 navel orange*

*3 walnuts (in the shell)*

*3 miniature corn (blue or strawberry)*

*twenty 3-inch lengths of cinnamon stick*

*3 small Lady apples*

*3 kumquats*

*shallow cardboard box*

*8-ounce can gold spray paint*

*drill with 1/64-inch bit*

*7-foot length 24-gauge florist's wire*

*sprigs of prostrate rosemary (approximately 7 feet total)*

## The Garland

1. Gild the pomegranates with gold spray paint as described in the box on page 17.

2. Cut the orange into 1/4-inch slices.

3. Using drill, make holes through walnuts, mini-corns, and gilded pomegranates.

4. Knot the 7-foot strand of 24-gauge florist's wire at one end.

5. In the following sequence, string the florist's wire with the garland ingredients: walnut, cinnamon stick, apple, cinnamon stick, kumquat, cinnamon stick, pomegranate, cinnamon stick, miniature corn, cinnamon stick, orange slice, cinnamon stick. Repeat procedure until garland is completed, then tie off end.

6. Hang garland in desired location.

7. Wrap lengths of rosemary around the garland.

# CHRISTMAS EVE WREATH

The Advent Wreath that graces our supper throughout the season takes on a slightly changed form on Christmas Eve. That is the day all our relatives come over for a traditional evening meal, with its wealth of savory fish courses. My favorites are the shrimp and scallops, baked with winter savory, oregano, and Italian parsley; poached salmon in a delicious lemony dill and fennel sauce; and baked calamari infused with Marie's special blend of lemon verbena, dill, savory, and parsley. Accompanying the feast are steaming bowls of thin spaghetti seasoned with garlic, oregano, and thyme and tossed with chopped pine nuts, filberts, walnuts, and anchovies. Herbs thus serve to flavor and enhance one of our most cherished family traditions. (For recipes, see pages 70–71.)

For this occasion, I replace the purple and pink candles in the Advent wreath with four pure white candles. In the spirit of joyful celebration, I add a small arrangement of white roses, white daisies, and eucalyptus to the center of the wreath.

For instructions on how to make the wreath, see Advent Wreath, page 63.

## MAKING THE ARRANGEMENT

1. Force a piece of wet floral foam into the bowl, and place the bowl in the center circle of the wreath.

2. Arrange the eucalyptus and foliage from the roses so that they hide the bowl and floral foam when the arrangement is completed.

3. Fill in with the roses and daisies.

## WHAT YOU WILL NEED

*1 dozen stems of eucalyptus*

*1 dozen white roses*

*1 dozen white daisies*

*4 white candles*

*4- to 5-inch-wide low bowl and a piece of floral foam cut to fit*

## Marie's Sautéed Shrimp or Scallops

### Ingredients

5 pounds large shrimp (12–
15 per pound), in shells

1 head of garlic, chopped

1 cup virgin olive oil

⅓ cup minced fresh savory
and oregano combined

1 cup minced fresh Italian
or flat-leaf parsley

1 teaspoon crushed red
pepper

1. Wash shrimp well. Drain in colander.

2. In a super-large skillet, sauté garlic in oil over medium heat for several minutes. Add the shrimp and
all the herbs and red pepper. Cover to steam, stir-
ring occasionally. Cook for 15 to 20 minutes, or until
shrimp is pink. Serve.

**NOTE:** This recipe may also be made using 5 pounds
sea scallops. Rinse and drain the scallops first, and
then follow the same recipe as for shrimp, *except*
eliminate the red pepper, and cook for only 5 to 10
minutes, or until scallops are just opaque. Drain and
serve.

## Christmas Eve Spaghetti

### Ingredients

1 cup virgin olive oil

1 head garlic, chopped

1 cup shelled chopped
filberts

1 cup shelled chopped
walnuts

¼ cup pine nuts

½ cup raisins

8 cups water

3 cans anchovies
(undrained)

⅓ cup minced fresh thyme
and oregano

3 pounds thin spaghetti
(vermicelli)

1. Pour olive oil into 8-quart pan, and sauté garlic over
medium heat until it is soft.

2. Add all the nuts and the raisins. Stir just a minute,
until raisins puff.

3. Add the water, anchovies, and herbs. Simmer for 45
minutes.

4. Cook the vermicelli in boiling water until tender but
still firm to the bite.

5. In a large pasta bowl, pour two or three ladles of
the sauce. Drain off vermicelli and transfer to the
bowl. Pour the remainder of the sauce over and
toss. Serve.

## CHRISTMAS EVE BAKED CALAMARI

1. Preheat oven to 375°F.

2. Mix all herbs (including garlic) and oil together in mixing bowl.

3. Wash and drain calamari and spread in large baking dish. Pour herb mix over and stir well, so that all of calamari has been thoroughly covered with herbs. Pepper to taste.

4. Bake, covered, for 15 minutes. Remove cover, and stir. Return uncovered dish to oven and cook for another 20 minutes. Serve hot.

### INGREDIENTS

*¼ cup bruised fresh lemon verbena leaves (or lemon balm)*

*¼ cup minced fresh dill*

*¼ cup minced fresh savory (or oregano)*

*½ cup minced fresh flat-leaf parsley*

*1 head garlic, chopped*

*¼ cup virgin olive oil*

*4 pounds cleaned calamari, cut in ½-inch-wide rings*

*crushed red pepper to taste*

*freshly ground black pepper to taste*

## BROILED SALMON IN LEMONY DILL AND FENNEL SAUCE

1. Preheat oven to 350°F.

2. Mix lemon juice and all herbs in oblong baking dish or broiler pan. Wash and drain salmon and place in dish. Turn fillet several times until fully covered with herb mix. With skin side down, pour olive oil over salmon. Sprinkle with freshly ground pepper.

3. Bake 5 to 10 minutes. Remove from oven and baste heavily with pan juices. Do not turn fillet. Raise oven temperature to broil and broil for another 5 minutes. Serve hot.

### INGREDIENTS

*3 pound salmon fillet*

*juice from two fresh-squeezed lemons*

*8 shallots, minced*

*¼ cup minced fresh dill*

*¼ cup minced fresh fennel*

*¼ cup olive oil*

*freshly ground black pepper to taste*

---

*A note on yield: These recipes, served along with several other main dishes, make enough for 30–35 people.*

# CANDELABRA WITH FRUITS AND ROSEMARY

For the Gilbertie family, the day after Christmas is a quiet time. Friends and neighbors often drop by, so we prepare a kind of self-serve high herbal tea that goes on all afternoon.

We put out teapot, cups, and saucers in an attractive setting along with fruits, cookies, and sweets, like a plum tart, against the backdrop of our lush herbal wreath. Family members and guests choose from the offerings as they wish.

Herbs, of course, are highly appropriate decorations for a tea table. The curves of the antique sterling silver candelabra that has been in our family for many years particularly lend themselves to embellishment with sprigs of the sprawling grower, prostrate rosemary. Many gardeners like to show off this variety by planting it in a hanging basket. If you do so, bring it inside in the fall and hang it in a sunny window. Then, when the time comes, you'll have plenty of long stems to work with for Christmas decorations.

To make the prostrate rosemary flower for Christmas, stop fertilizing it after November and keep it in the coolest yet brightest spot in the house.

## DECORATING THE CANDELABRA

1. Wrap two strands of rosemary around the arms of the candelabra, beginning at opposite ends.

2. Wrap one strand around the center candle, being sure to put the glue on the strand before making it adhere to the wax candle.

3. Glue clusters of red cranberries onto the rosemary at both ends and in the middle.

4. Place glue on kumquats, then fasten them to the candelabra.

## WHAT YOU WILL NEED

*three 12-inch strands prostrate rosemary*

*⅛ cup freeze-dried red cranberries*

*2 kumquats*

*candelabra*

*hot glue gun and glue sticks*

*candles*

CHAPTER 6

# *Highlighting Special Places*

*A*treasured family heirloom, such as an antique spinning
wheel or a handmade country basket, can make a surprisingly effective backdrop for herbal decorations during the
holidays. Allow the object to dictate how your dried herbs
and other materials may be used for embellishment. Special places in the house — a staircase landing, a fireplace
mantel, a window seat or other alcove — also make excellent staging areas for a crèche or some other scene of
Christmas past, present, or future.

*⇐Lamp post trimmed with hemlock and artemisia 'Silver King'*

# Living Room Mantel

Graced with cedar, herbs, gilded pomegranates, and pine cones, and illuminated with candlelight, the mantel in our living room is the site of a short-lived but pleasing spectacle every year. Sometimes we light the candles on Christmas Eve, sometimes on Christmas night, depending on when we'll be spending several hours in the room. They offer a wonderful glow when guests are over, or when Marie and I manage to steal some time just to sit and talk.

The fireplace mantel itself came from an old Vermont barn, but even this rustic timber achieves a certain elegance with the addition of greenery, brass candlesticks, and white beeswax candles. Complementing the off-white of the candles, a hearthside basket overflows with dried white strawflowers, golden flax, natural poppy pods, and silver lamb's-ears.

## Decorating the Mantel

1. Gild the pomegranates following directions in box, page 17.

2. Arrange candles and candlesticks so that the tallest tapers are on the flanks.

3. Interweave cedar, holly, and dried herbs among the candles.

4. Place gilded pomegranates and pine cones atop the greenery at the bases of candles. (Use glue gun, if necessary.)

## What You Will Need

*20 dried pomegranates*

*twelve 12-inch lengths silver cedar (such as 'Blue Atlas')*

*twelve 12-inch lengths green holly*

*12 stems dried lamb's-ears*

*12 stems dried 'Silver King' artemisia*

*12 pine cones*

*shallow cardboard box*

*8-ounce can gold spray paint*

*twelve 10-inch beeswax tapers*

*four 3-inch, four 4-inch, and four 6-inch beeswax candles (3-inch diameter)*

*12 assorted brass and glass candleholders*

*hot glue gun and glue sticks*

# FAMILY ROOM MANTEL

With a blazing fire and a collection of St. Nicks to one side, it's no surprise that the hearth in our family room is a major focal point and gathering place on Christmas Eve. This is the room where herbs from our gardens hang in bunches year-round, so the herbal arrangement I make for the fireplace has to be something special to stand out.

A combination of holly, juniper, and lamb's-ears arranged in a fanlike pattern brings together the traditional Christmas colors of red, green, silver, and even gold (in the variegated juniper). It's an appealing backdrop for the children's Christmas stockings, filled with simple but welcome surprises and topped with fruit.

## FAN OF GREENS AND HERBS

1. Use nails and florist's wire to secure several branches of juniper to the wall above the mantel in an erect position, keeping in mind your final fan-shape pattern.

2. Use florist's wire to secure the holly branches to the juniper.

3. Tuck lamb's-ears stems into the juniper and holly, continuing to follow the established fan-shape pattern. (They will easily stay in place without tying.)

### WHAT YOU WILL NEED

*six 24-inch juniper boughs (Juniperus procumbens 'Variegata', if possible)*

*ten 24-inch sprays of green holly*

*100 stems dried lamb's-ears*

*12 finishing nails or heavy-gauge tacks (1½-inch)*

*1 standard roll 24-gauge florist's wire*

*Lamb's-ears*

# HEARTH BUCKETFUL OF HERBS

One reason the cast-iron bucket is found next to the fireplace in our family room throughout the year is that it is so heavy to move — at least 120 pounds. A friend gave it to us years ago after finding it at a tag sale. Actually, it gets lots of use during the winter months, principally as a container for kindling and old newspapers. At Christmas, I like to dress it up with dried herbs and evergreens, so that it echoes the colors and textures of the mantelpiece arrangement and the bunches of dried herbs hanging from the beams overhead.

## HERB BUCKET

1. Force Styrofoam base into the bucket, so that it is secure.

2. Place green holly and 'Blue Atlas' cedar at wide intervals in the Styrofoam base.

3. Randomly insert stems of dried poppy pods and lamb's-ears.

4. Fill in with stems of red chili peppers and dried statice, as needed.

## WHAT YOU WILL NEED

*eight 24-inch stems green holly*

*six 18-inch stems silver cedar (such as 'Blue Atlas')*

*24 stems dried poppy pods*

*12 stems dried lamb's-ears*

*6 stems dried red chili peppers*

*2 bunches dried statice*

*large bucket or other appropriate container*

*1 sheet Styrofoam, 2 inch × 12 inch × 12 inch, or size needed to fit securely into bucket*

# WINDOWBOX CRÈCHE

My living herbal crèche is basically a wood planter that
I keep in our south-facing bay window. Amid the rosemary, sweet myrtle, lavender, thyme, silver curry plant,
and sweet olive I set the hickory-bark manger that our son
Tom made for us one Christmas. I fashioned the Infant
Jesus from raffia, with a nigella pod for the head and a
yellow strawflower for the halo. The sheep are made from
the stems, leaves, and flowers of lamb's-ears, with cloves
for the eyes.

After the holiday season, when the crèche is removed, the herbs in the planter continue to flourish, and we enjoy their fragrances and flavors throughout the winter months.

Sometimes I put our crèche in the living room or family room for the Christmas season and use the planter in the bay window as the setting for a collection of miniature ceramic Victorian houses. Interspersed with the herbs and added boughs of holly, the houses take on the atmosphere of a New England village.

The bay window has a lovely view of fields and woods, so it's a natural focal point for an herbal Christmas. I like to put a hand-carved Santa Claus and sleigh just outside, so that we can enjoy them from inside the house, especially when there's fresh snow on the ground.

## CREATING THE CRÈCHE

If you follow a simple technique I learned years ago, it's fairly simple to construct any basic form from dried flowers and herbs. First, sketch the figure or form in actual size. Then, using the selected dried herbs available, lay them out on the rough sketch. This method usually allows you to immediately establish the pattern, as well as the order in which you will assemble or glue the herbs and flowers together. This is exactly the method I use to construct the sheep for the crèche scene. I cut up three or four lamb's-ears flower heads into tiny pieces, and lay them out on the drawing, arranging those at the sheep's head so that they form a natural-looking nose and face. I use cloves for eyes, several small leaves for the ears, and four stems for the legs. When everything is in place, I quickly glue them all together. This is so easy to do and so much fun that children may enjoy doing this project with you. (Do not allow children to use a glue gun unsupervised.)

To make the manger and the tiny figure of the Infant Jesus, follow the directions on the next page.

## The Manger

1. To make the manger, form two perfect Xs with the 3-inch stems, and glue each together at their crossings.

2. Join the two Xs by gluing the three 5-inch stems to the inside of the upper part of the Xs, with one stem at the crossing and the other two stems at the upper arms, to form a manger.

3. Glue pieces of straw or dried grass diagonally inside the manger.

4. To make the tiny figure, gather a handful of natural raffia and fold it over several times into a package about 4 inches long and about 1 inch around. Wrap it neatly with a separate piece of raffia to form a little bundle for the body. To form the wider shoulders, wrap more loosely at the top of the body and spread the raffia with your fingers.

5. Glue the nigella pod on top of the body to make the head. Glue the yellow strawflower behind the head to form the halo.

6. Glue or set the figure in cradle.

### What You Will Need

*4 firm stems of any dried herb, such as mint, lamb's-ears, or yarrow, each cut 3 inches long*

*3 stems of the same or other dried herbs, cut 5 inches long*

*small handful of straw or dried grass*

*handful of natural raffia*

*1 nigella pod*

*1 yellow strawflower, 1-inch diameter*

*hot glue gun and glue sticks*

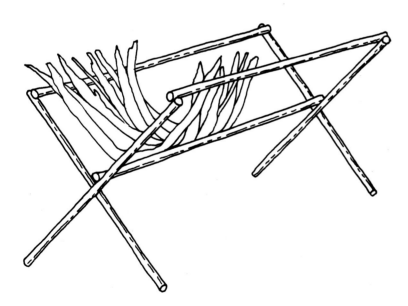

*The manger, made of herbs and straw, and the figure of the Infant Jesus, made of raffia and dried flowers.*

# THE PEACEABLE KINGDOM

The serenity of the peaceable kingdom — the promise inherent in the Christmas story — is captured in our lion and lamb figures crafted by a talented designer and friend. Against a background of dried herbs and flowers that evokes spring and summer in the middle of winter, the creatures provide a tableau that seems to captivate everyone who comes into our house during the holidays. Measuring four feet across and set on top of the armoire that greets visitors as they walk into the family room, the arrangement is truly a show-stopper.

The animal figures for this piece could be made of fabric, ceramic, or other material, but I wanted my lion and lamb to be all herbal. The lion's coat is golden yarrow, with a mane and tail made of raffia. Its face is white pearly everlasting and its nose and mouth are red cockscomb. The lamb is made entirely of dried lamb's-ears, with a speck of pink cockscomb for the nose and mouth and a pair of cloves for eyes.

## CREATING THE LION AND LAMB

The lion and lamb figures are a rather lengthy project — don't expect to create these in one evening. They make a wonderful craft for when you want to prepare for the coming holidays in the late summer or early fall months.

1. Both figures are made on a papier-mâché form. To construct your own, use a kitchen knife to carve out the shapes of each animal from several blocks of floral foam. You will need five blocks for the lion and one for the lamb. Glue pieces together as you carve the shapes. (See drawing, page 12.)

2. Once you are satisfied with the forms, make a light paste of flour and water — the consistency of soup. Add a teaspoon of salt. Soak paper towels in the solution, then spread them onto the form. Pat the paper towels carefully into every crevice. Set to dry for twenty-four hours.

## WHAT YOU WILL NEED FOR THE LION AND LAMB

*18–24 large heads of dried golden yarrow*

*1 large head dried red cockscomb*

*8 stems of dried pearly everlasting*

*10–12 heads of dried lamb's-ears*

*2 dried lamb's-ears leaves*

*1 small piece dried pink cockscomb*

*2 cloves*

*6 blocks of dry floral foam, 9" x 4" x 3"*

*kitchen knife*

*½ cup flour*

*water*

*1 teaspoon salt*

*paper towels*

*2 glass eyes*

*1 pound natural raffia*

3. For a quick sense of accomplishment, glue on the glass eyes first.

4. Cut the yarrow heads from their stems, and then cut all the tiny stems apart from the head. This will leave you with small clusters of yarrow flowers. The tedious job of gluing these onto the body of the lion will take several hours, so it may be a good idea to plan on several "seatings" for this project. Cover the form completely with the yarrow.

5. Glue on pieces of cockscomb for the nose and mouth, and the pearly-everlasting flowers for the face.

6. Take eight or ten 15-inch lengths of raffia, and braid them into a tail. Leave the last 3 or 4 inches unbraided for the hair effect. Cut the end of the braid neatly and glue it into place on the lion's backside.

7. Cut 3-, 4-, and 5-inch lengths of raffia, and glue them into a pattern around the back of the lion's head to form a mane.

8. To complete the lamb, cut up the lamb's-ears flowers into tiny pieces, and glue them over the entire form to create a wool effect for the lamb's body.

9. Cut the tips of the dried lamb's-ear leaves to form the ears, and glue in place.

10. Break up the pink cockscomb into tiny pieces, and shape the lamb's mouth.

11. Glue in the two cloves for the eyes.

## CREATING THE SETTING

Make an upright arrangement of the dried plant materials to serve as a background for the figures by inserting the dried sunflowers in a line at the back of the flat Styrofoam base. In front of the sunflowers, secure the stems of wheat, mountain mint, and oregano. In front of these, place the red roses, cockscomb, yarrows, and strawflowers. Fill in any empty spaces with baby's-breath and dried grasses as needed, and place lion and lamb figures as desired.

### WHAT YOU WILL NEED FOR THE SETTING

*12 dried long-stemmed sunflowers (4–6-inch heads)*

*1 bunch dried wheat (50 stems)*

*2 bunches dried mountain mint (40 stems)*

*2 bunches dried oregano (40 stems)*

*12 stems dried red roses*

*12 stems dried red cockscomb*

*8 stems dried yellow yarrow*

*12 stems dried white yarrow*

*15 stems dried yellow strawflowers*

*50 small clusters dried baby's-breath*

*2 small bunches dried grasses*

*2-inch x 12-inch x 24-inch sheet green Styrofoam*

*lion figure*

*lamb figure*

# SPINNING WHEEL HERBS

One Christmas a few years ago, Marie mentioned to me that she thought our antique spinning wheel, which originally came from a convent in Connecticut, looked a little plain and forlorn in a living room that was otherwise all dressed up for the holidays. My first thought was simply to put the spinning wheel in the attic for a few weeks, but then I had a better idea. Why not decorate it with dried herbs to make it look a little as if it were spinning yarn again?

## TRIMMING THE WHEEL

1. Tie wheel in place so it will not rotate.

2. Run twine from wheel to spindle and tie securely.

3. Tie thinnest tips of artemisia to twine with florist's wire.

4. Tie artemisia, oregano, and anise hyssop to rim of wheel.

5. Attach a loose cluster of artemisia to hub of wheel.

6. Using glue gun, affix globe amaranth heads throughout the decoration.

## WHAT YOU WILL NEED

*5 bunches dried 'Silver King' artemisia (100 stems)*

*2 bunches dried oregano (40 stems)*

*1 bunch dried anise hyssop (12 stems)*

*100 heads dried red globe amaranth*

*spinning wheel*

*12–15 feet strong twine*

*fifty 18-inch lengths 26-gauge florist's wire*

*hot glue gun and glue sticks*

# Herbal Topiary Corner

It takes time and patience to grow healthy herbal topiaries, so a gardener can't be blamed for showing off some of his prized possessions at Christmas, can he?

There's a corner in our den that receives perfect winter light for nurturing plants, and that's where I locate my topiary stand. With Christmas on hand, Marie gathers some of her favorite ornaments and transforms the stand full of santolina, myrtle, thyme, rosemary, and prostrate rosemary into a cheerful and perky corner. Lavender, curry plant, and silver teucrium also make great herbal topiaries and are usually available in garden centers and herb shops.

Keeping herbal topiaries during the winter months is quite simple, provided you have direct bright light — either a southern or western exposure will do. It's a good idea to turn your topiaries every other day so that both sides get equal sun.

Most topiaries should also be watered every other day in the average home, but since each home differs in temperature and humidity, you may need to create your own watering schedule. Never, however, let a topiary completely dry out.

Fertilize every other week with a liquid organic fertilizer, such as fish emulsion.

Trimming your topiaries begins as the individual branches start to grow. Use sharp pruning scissors to trim and shape, keeping in mind the specific form you wish to achieve. This care and attention to maintaining your topiary's shape adds to the fun and satisfaction, even though you may sometimes feel like a hairdresser.

CHAPTER 7

# Finishing
# Touches

Small enough in size to be very manageable and at the
same time so visually appealing, herbs make a good
material for decorating light fixtures, small tables, and
other nooks and crannies. Such herbal detailing serves to
link the major arrangements and create a festive atmosphere in every room. Prostrate rosemary, for example,
with its slightly unruly growing habit, is a source for
graceful strands of aromatic greens to set off a wall sconce
or candelabra (see pages 103 and 105).

# BERIBBONED HANGING APPLES

Polished apples are my secret ingredient for bringing the bright red of Christmas into the house during the holidays. I hang them from the fireplace mantel, from the wood beams in the family room, and from arched doorways. Apples are like herbs — wholesome, fun, universally accepted. Our holiday visitors invariably get a kick out of seeing the apples used in such a playful decorative fashion. And, when the decorations come down in early January, the apples are tossed out under the grape arbor for the deer and squirrels.

## The Apples

1. Polish the apples with a soft towel.

2. Cut ribbon into 12- to 15-inch lengths.

3. To attach ribbon and a sprig of lamb's-ears to each apple at the same time, push a sheetrock nail firmly through the plant material and ribbon and into the fruit at the stem end.

4. Hang apples by ribbons at desired lengths using thumbtacks. Cut off excess ribbon above tack.

### What You Will Need

*small red apples (about 1 bushel Macoun, McIntosh, or Red Delicious)*

*sprigs of lamb's-ears*

*1 roll 1½-inch ribbon (25 yards)*

*100 sheetrock nails (1½-inch)*

*box of thumbtacks, matching color of ribbon*

# HALL TABLE WITH HERBAL SWAG

An otherwise ordinary table and mirror in a hall or spare room can be the setting for a holiday vision with the simple addition of dried herbs and flowers arranged in a thoughtful manner. I try to coordinate our entry hall with the decorative theme of the front porch, so that's why I've included an angel, the gilded pomegranates, and the fruit. This arrangement is suitable, however, for any room in the house.

## PITCHER AND BOWL

1. Spray pomegranates with gold paint, following instructions in box on page 17.

2. Place eucalyptus in pitcher in a loose arrangement.

3. Add the rose stems.

4. Carefully insert small bunches of baby's-breath into empty spaces between roses.

5. Fill the bowl with apples and pomegranates.

## WHAT YOU WILL NEED

*8 dried pomegranates*

*12 stems 'Spiral' eucalyptus*

*3 dozen stems dried pink and red roses*

*24 small bunches dried baby's-breath*

*20 small red apples*

*shallow cardboard box*

*8-ounce can gold spray paint*

*Gilded pomegranates*

## What You Will Need

*10 dried pomegranates*

*1 bunch 'Spiral' eucalyptus (20 stems)*

*18 small bunches dried baby's-breath*

*shallow cardboard box*

*8-ounce can gold spray paint*

*1 standard roll 24-gauge florist's wire*

*hot glue gun and glue sticks*

*angel figure*

*picture hanger*

## SWAG OVER MIRROR

1. Spray pomegranates with gold paint, following instructions in box on page 17.

2. Set out two 12- to 15-inch stems of eucalyptus in opposite directions, and tie them together securely with florist's wire. Repeat three to five times. Tie the entire spray together as shown.

3. Using glue gun, secure pomegranates to eucalyptus in a symmetrical pattern, leaving space at the center for the angel figure.

4. Fill in empty spaces by gluing short pieces of eucalyptus and baby's-breath to the spray.

5. Attach the angel to the spray with florist's wire.

**6.** Affix a picture hanger to the wall above the mirror. Attach the spray to the hanger with a wire loop on back of the spray.

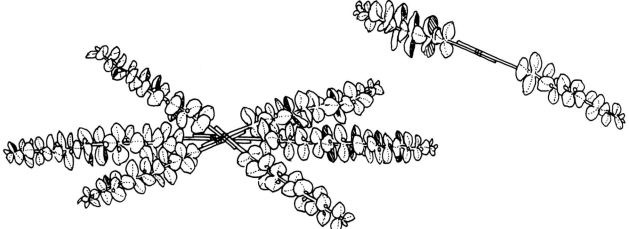

*Wiring the eucalyptus*

# WALL SCONCE WITH FRUITS, HERBS, AND GREENS

*

A wall sconce is easy to decorate with herbs — a graceful touch for the Christmas house with very little effort. I like to coordinate the pair of sconces in our dining room with the decorative elements in the herbal wreath and the candelabra on the table we use for serving food (see pages 63 and 105). The materials listed are enough to decorate one sconce.

## WALL SCONCE

1. Use the piece of cardboard to protect the work surface. Set out twenty to twenty-five dried cranberries in a 4-inch semicircle (the shape of a half moon). With a glue gun, apply glue so that berries adhere to one another in the crescent shape. Apply more glue to the top of these berries, and add more berries. Repeat process until cluster of cranberries is about an inch high. (See drawing, page 12.)

2. Place the cranberry cluster at the base of the candle on the sconce. Secure apple to top of cranberry cluster with hot glue.

3. Add bay, thyme, and lamb's-ears to the base of the sconce. Place kumquats on top, using glue gun to secure, if necessary. (If you need to glue the fruit to the candle, put glue on the fruit first, and then press it firmly to the candle.)

4. Tuck sprays of holly behind the candle.

5. Wrap rosemary around the candle, securing to holly with florist's wire, if necessary.

## WHAT YOU WILL NEED

*⅛ cup freeze-dried cranberries*

*2 sprigs each: bay, thyme, and lamb's-ears (dried)*

*3 small kumquats*

*1 small Lady apple*

*three 8-inch stems green holly*

*three 10-inch strands prostrate rosemary*

*12-inch x 18-inch piece of cardboard*

*hot glue gun and glue sticks*

*18-inch length 26-gauge florist's wire*

# CHANDELIER TRIMMED WITH CRANBERRY RINGS AND CINNAMON STICKS

My final arrangement of the holiday season is the garlands for the chandelier in the dining room. I like to save it for last to coincide with the traditional Christmas Eve dinner we host for family and friends every year. My father-in-law, Anthony, and I usually assemble it at the last minute in my basement while the somewhat frenzied preparations for the feast are underway in the kitchen. There is always a bit of tension about whether or not the chandelier will actually be decorated by the time people sit down for dinner, but over two decades we have made the deadline every time. The materials listed are enough for one three-foot garland.

## GARLAND FOR CHANDELIER

1. Use the piece of cardboard to protect the work surface. Set out dried cranberries in four 1½-inch-wide circles of twenty to twenty-five berries each. With a glue gun, apply glue so that each cluster of berries adheres as a unit. (See drawing, page 12.)

2. Using the drill, make holes in the walnuts.

3. With nail or ice pick, poke holes through centers of kumquats, Lady apples, and cranberry clusters.

4. Cut an 8-foot strand of 24-gauge florist's wire and knot at one end.

5. In the following sequence, string the florist's wire with the following ingredients: walnut, cinnamon stick, kumquat, cinnamon stick, cranberry cluster, cinnamon stick, lady apple, cinnamon stick. Repeat this

### WHAT YOU WILL NEED

*½ cup freeze-dried cranberries*

*4 walnuts (in the shell)*

*4 kumquats*

*4 lady apples*

*eighteen 1-inch cinnamon sticks*

*15–20 stems 'Spiral' eucalyptus*

*one 15-inch x 18-inch piece of cardboard*

*hot glue gun and glue sticks*

*drill with ¹⁄₆₄-inch bit*

*2-inch nail or ice pick*

*1 standard roll 24-gauge florist's wire*

sequence until the garland is completed, then tie off the end.

6. Wrap the garland around each arm of the chandelier. Use florist's wire to secure.

7. Secure eucalyptus stems to the chandelier in a pleasing pattern with florist's wire.

8. Fill the candle cups with loose freeze-dried cranberries.

*Cinnamon sticks*

# Appendix

## Plants Used in Projects

| Common Name | Botanical Name | Plant type |
|---|---|---|
| Amaranth, globe | *Gomphrena globosa* 'Pink' | A |
| Amaranth, globe | *Gomphrena* 'Strawberry Fields' | A |
| Anise hyssop | *Agastache foeniculum* | P |
| Artemisia — 'Silver King' | *Artemisia ludoviciana* 'Silver King' | P |
| Artemisia — narrow leaf | *Artemisia ludoviciana* var. *albula* | P |
| Artemisia — 'Valerie Finnis' | *Artemisia ludoviciana* 'Valerie Finnis' | P |
| Artemisia — 'Silver Queen' | *Artemisia ludoviciana* 'Silver Queen' | P |
| Balm — golden lemon | *Melissa officinalis aurea* | P |
| Basil — cinnamon | *Ocimum basilicum* 'Cinnamon' | P |
| Bay | *Laurus nobilis* | TP |
| Chili pepper | *Capsicum annuum* | A |
| Cockscomb | *Celosia cristata* | A |
| Curry plant | *Helichrysum angustifolium* | TP |
| Eucalyptus — 'Spiral' | *Eucalyptus cinerea* 'Spiral' | TP |
| Flax | *Linum usitatissimum* | A |
| Hyssop — blue | *Hyssopus officinalis* | P |
| Lamb's-ears | *Stachys byzantina* | P |
| Lavender — fringed | *Lavandula dentata* | TP |
| Lavender — latifolia | *Lavandula latifolia* | P |
| Lavender | *Lavandula angustifolia* | P |
| Mint — mountain, broad leaf | *Pycnanthemum muticum* | P |
| Mint — mountain, narrow leaf | *Pycnanthemum virginianum* | P |
| Oregano | *Origanum* species | P |
| Pearly everlasting | *Anaphalis triplinervis* | P |
| Poppy | *Papaver* species | A |
| Rosemary | *Rosmarinus officinalis* | TP |

| Common Name | Botanical Name | Plant type |
|---|---|---|
| Rosemary — 'Arp' | *Rosmarinus officinalis* 'Arp' | TP |
| Rosemary — prostrate | *Rosmarinus officinalis* 'Prostratus' | TP |
| Russian sage | *Perovskia atriplicifolia* | P |
| Sage — golden | *Salvia officinalis* 'Aurea' | P |
| Sage — purple | *Salvia officinalis* 'Purpurea' | P |
| Sage — tricolored | *Salvia officinalis* 'Tricolor' | P |
| Santolina — green | *Santolina rosmarinifolia* | P |
| Santolina — gray | *Santolina chamaecyparissus* | P |
| Scotch broom | *Cytisus scoparius* | P |
| Silver teucrium | *Teucrium fruticans* | TP |
| Southernwood | *Artemisia abrotanum* | P |
| Southernwood — tangerine | *Artemisia abrotanum* 'Tangerine' | P |
| Statice — pinks and lavenders | *Limonium sinuatum* | A |
| Thyme — golden lemon | *Thymus* x *citriodorus* 'Aureus' | P |
| Thyme — silver | *Thymus vulgaris variegata* | P |
| Wormwood | *Artemisia absinthium* | P |
| Yarrow — white (sneezewort) | *Achillea ptarmica* 'The Pearl' | P |
| Yarrow — yellow | *Achillea filipendulina* | P |

**Key: A = annual; P = perennial; TP = tender perennial**

# CREDITS

A special thank you for those who provided accessories for photography:  Marilyn Allen; Marcia Alvord — Every Blooming Thing, South Norwalk, CT; Nicholas and Timothy Anderson; Julie Doetsch; John and Sarah Jaeger; Tom Johnson — Lexington Gardens, Newtown, CT; Dora Jonassen; Angela Miller; Lisa Moser; Coleen O'Shea; Ruth O'Shea; Osborne and Little; Patrick Padula —  Olde Well Antiques, South Norwalk, CT; Cathryn Schwing; Slady's Apple Farm, Easton, CT; Joseph Totora; Bob Weiss

# *Index*

Page numbers in *italics* indicate illustrations.